Excerpts from *Money Secrets of the Zodiac*:

About Cancer: *"Deep down, you never really feel that you have enough money to satisfy your desire for financial security for yourself and your loved ones."*

Aquarius and Capricorn Relationship: *As much as Capricorn would like to have Aquarius think 'inside the Capricorn box', it is improbable that Aquarius can willingly adapt to the money expectations of Capricorn.*

About Gemini: *"There just does not seem to be enough hours in the day to execute all your brilliant ideas, in particular taking the time to invest the cash that is sitting in your checking account."*

Leo Investment Advice: *"Keep your investment decisions to yourself as then your personal pride will not come into play and you will keep a clear and logical mind."*

Pisces Money Tip: *"Avoid being swayed by your emotions to give funds to those in need who in reality have the ability to help themselves."*

Aries and Libra Relationship: *"This can be a one-sided money relationship, as Aries can be too self-assertive and forceful for Libra to be able to express money concerns."*

Scorpio's Money Viewpoint: *"Money reveals the inner greed in people and their degree of caring for others."*

MONEY SECRETS

of the

ZODIAC

by
Stephanie Venn

This book is dedicated to my daughter Alexis.

ACKNOWLEDGMENTS

I would like to express my gratitude to all the wonderful clients I have served over the years. A special thanks to Jimmy P. Lewis, filmmaker extraordinaire, for his encouragement to write this book.

TABLE OF CONTENTS

INTRODUCTION

CHAPTER 1

CHAPTER 2

CHAPTER 3

CHAPTER 4

INTRODUCTION

I believe that money can assist us in living up to our potential. It is with this positive point of view that I wrote this book. Some people need very little money to be able to live satisfying lives and others never seem to have enough to feel secure. We truly are different when it comes to money needs and attitudes.

I have been in wealth management for several years advising clients primarily in the area of investment management.   My clients, which often included all family members, were varied as to backgrounds, age, assets, occupations, and in their attitudes towards money. Some had no knowledge of and no interest in learning about managing their money and I had the discretionary authority to make investment decisions on their behalf.   Others were well versed in financial matters and were eager to team with me when making investment decisions.

This book is meant to open the door of your consciousness to the variety of money personalities that emerge from the depths of people's brains. It may give you an understanding of why people react the way they do when it comes to money matters and how to use this knowledge as an aid when making financial decisions. I had learned in my career as a financial advisor that you have to accept an individual's core money values without bias in order to formulate and communicate appropriate advice.

You do *not have to believe in astrology* for this book to be meaningful to you. Basically, there are twelve different personality types described in this book. The reason why I have chosen to use the Zodiac archetypes is that no other 'personality classification' system seems to be as complete to me in describing human nature. The Zodiac Signs represent archetypal mindsets that are just as valid in the modern world as they were in ancient times.

CHAPTER 1

THE ZODIAC SIGNS

Over 2,000 years ago, the ancients named 12 star clusters that could be seen by the naked eye in the night skies. These constellations surround the ecliptic path, the great circular road in space that the Earth travels to orbit the Sun over the course of 12 months. The star groupings became known as the Zodiac and were named in sequential order as they circled the celestial globe. The ancients started this Zodiac sequence with the Sign Aries, a specific cluster of stars that they saw as a backdrop in the sky at sunrise on the day of the spring solstice. As the day progressed and the earth turned around its axis, the backdrop of the sky moved to Taurus and so on to Pisces and then arrived back at Aries.

Each one of the 12 Zodiac Signs were assigned personal characteristics over the years that described unique human traits. If you could put all of these traits together into one individual, you would have created a person that was so well-rounded that he or she could deal with any type of life challenges, such as *money* issues.

For those of you with an interest in astrology, the money personalities described in this book are *not necessarily the person's Sun Sign*. A person may have stronger planetary forces converging in their 'Second Astrological House of Money' that could overpower the influence of the Sun Sign when it comes to money.

As well, your so-called natal Sun Sign may not be what you think it is since it was likely assigned using ancient tropical time as opposed to modern astronomical **sidereal** time. You can refer to the Table below if you would like to reference your Sun Sign using the day of your birth and the *actual* location of the Sun in the sky at that time.

Here are the Sun Signs using sidereal placement of the Sun for your day of your birth. Note that two Signs can fall on the same day as the Sun is transitioning to the next sign. *(For more information on sidereal astrology, visit **www.sidscopes.com**.)*

Aries	Apr 14 - May 15
Taurus	May 15 - June 15
Gemini	June 15 - July 17
Cancer	July 17 - Aug 17
Leo	Aug 17 - Sept 18
Virgo	Sept 18 - Oct 18
Libra	Oct 18 - Nov 17
Scorpio	Nov 17 - Dec 16
Sagittarius	Dec 16 - Jan 14
Capricorn	Jan 14 - Feb 13
Aquarius	Feb 13 - Mar 15
Pisces	Mar 15 - Apr 14

CHAPTER 2

SAVING AND SPENDING

THE DIFFERENT MONEY MINDSETS

Have you ever wondered why people can differ so much in their money needs and attitudes? For example, at one extreme some people are reluctant to spend and they consider their accumulating dollars as sacred pots of gold reserved for old age. On the other hand, some people have no interest in saving their money as they feel life is just too short and they might as well spend their money while the going is good and they can still dance. Who is to say who is right and who is wrong? It is very difficult to be objective if you are going to make judgment as your ego will immediately bring your own money personality and value system into play. Most would agree that having more money is better than having less. Most would agree that extreme money attitudes don't lead to proper financial decisions. Most people fall somewhere in between these two extremes.

What follows is a description of each Zodiac Sign and the way that Sign reacts with money. At the end of each description are some tips intended to keep that Sign on a positive money track. One personality type may resonate strongly with your own nature or you may feel like you are a combination of types.

ARIES AND MONEY

Aries as a Spender

Ready, set, go! With the Aries personality, there are no second thoughts when wanting to buy something. You want it, so why not just go get it and be done with it. It really doesn't matter what it costs and most times you don't bother looking at the price tag. Anything in your way, watch out as you will abruptly push it aside and leave it in your dust as you forge ahead. Few dare to challenge you when you are in action-mode as it is plain to see that you are determined and fearless. The faster you get what you intend to have, the closer you will be to be able to pursue other interests. You rarely have any regrets later on as to what you spent your money on.

Aries as a Saver

You really haven't given much thought to saving as you are too busy trying to take advantage of opportunities before the competition sets in. It seems that you always end up getting what you want most of the time so there is no point fretting about saving. With your willpower and drive, you can generate the funds when needed. Consequently, you have little concern if you do not have any significant savings.

Money Tips for Aries

- Listen to at least one friend's opinion before making a major financial decision.

- Create an automatic savings plan that systematically has funds transferred into it from your earnings.

- Have a serious review of what type of lifestyle you want to be able to achieve in retirement and have a formal financial plan prepared.

- If retired, before making a major purchase weigh the financial impact of this expenditure on your remaining savings to see how it will affect your ongoing lifestyle.

♉

TAURUS AND MONEY

Taurus as a Spender

With a Taurus personality you are likely not to talk about your purchases to anyone beforehand. There is no point in proclaiming your intentions and adding to the drama of the world. As far as you are concerned, there are already enough talkers adding to the madness. You may silently give away a clue, though, since you can't resist touching what you are thinking about buying if it is a physical good within your hands reach. You are easily swayed by sensory pleasures. There is nothing like the delicious cuisine served at your favorite restaurant. Despite these sensual lures, you are thrifty and practical with your money and you do not spend beyond your means. At the same time, you do indulge in luxuries when appropriate. You are proud of your possessions and they are a reflection of your admirable values. They have an enduring quality to them. Chances are that your life is made more comfortable and pleasing in some way when you spend your money.

Taurus as a Saver

You are determined in your efforts to accumulate wealth and it important to you to have sufficient savings. Your home and furnishings also represent important investments to you. Having an adequate amount of funds for retirement is definitely a priority as you cannot imagine yourself being uncomfortable or insecure at that stage of your life. You are very protective of your pot-of-gold as it is your security blanket.

Money Tips for Taurus

- Beware of the lure of luxuries.

- Entertain the opinions of others before making major financial decisions.

- Watch out for possessiveness that can lead to paranoia.

- For peace of mind, have a formal financial plan prepared.

- Accept that some people do not value possessions as much as you do and have more esoteric goals in life.

II

GEMINI AND MONEY

Gemini as a Spender

Needless to say to a Gemini, you have lots of ideas as to how to spend your money and you have many clever alternatives to satisfy your needs. You are always up for some brain-storming and conversation about where to go and buy whatever it may be. You can count on a Gemini to immediately search the internet on that product or service and make detailed comparisons as to what exactly fits the bill. As a Gemini, you may change your mind on your purchase at the last minute if something else comes up that checks out to be superior. At the same time it is unlikely that you get 'buyer's remorse' as your mind is quickly off pursuing other interests, of which there are ample in your world. You can always resort to your friends for their valuable input. You respect their opinions as generally they are pretty smart people, like yourself.

Gemini as a Saver

As quick as you are in figuring out ways to spend your money, you are also good at figuring out ways to save your money. Carrying out a savings plan is another matter though. There just does not seem to be enough hours in the day to execute all your brilliant ideas, in particular taking the time to invest the cash that is sitting in your checking account. You may end up spending more than you save if you don't transfer that money into savings and invest it.

Money Tips for Gemini

- Create an automatic savings plan that systematically has funds transferred into it from your earnings.

- Avoid setting up a multitude of financial accounts as it will only lead to confusion; consolidate your finances into one financial account so you can see the whole picture and manage it more effectively.

- Have a formal financial plan prepared to help you focus on your future needs.

- Conflicting financial advice can lead you to a state of inaction. Keep the best and leave the rest and get on with the program.

CANCER AND MONEY

Cancer as a Spender

When it comes to spending, with a Cancer personality you resist disclosing your needs and take your time deciding what you want. You generally make do with what money you have and are resourcefully thrifty. You like to buy things that make your home comfortable and enjoyable. Your home is your peaceful refuge and provides you with a deep sense of security. You get much pleasure from giving to family and friends, and it bothers you if you feel someone has been left out. Deep down, you never really feel that you have enough money to satisfy your desire for financial security for yourself and your loved ones.

Cancer as a Saver

You intuitively know that it is important to save as you want to feel that you are financially secure. You do listen to that inner reminder to save for a rainy day and set aside funds whenever you can. If you have children, you may have already planned to set aside funds for their future educational needs. You can have an attachment to money depending on where it was derived from. For example, if it was inherited from a cherished ancestor, you want those funds to be preserved and protected from reckless spending or risky investments.

Money Tips for Cancer

- Avoid attaching emotions to money; a dollar is just a dollar and has no special meaning based on where it originated.

- Remember to be generous with yourself and to splurge on an indulgence now and again.

- Don't let other people's money problems get you down; it is inevitable that we will all encounter some form of money difficulties that most can overcome on their own with good direction.

- Avoid being so generous such that it spoils the receiver's incentive to be self-supporting.

- For peace of mind, have a financial plan prepared. Let that person know of your strong need for financial security.

♌

LEO AND MONEY

Leo as a Spender

With a Leo personality, you don't think twice about laying out an enormous sum of money for, say, a car, but at the same time you are repulsed when something much less significant is priced a dollar more than it should be. You know what you like and waste little time acquiring it. You have a taste for luxury but you keep your eye out for sales. You will pay what is necessary to keep up your lifestyle, and you treasure royal comfort. You have to be careful not to have the price of your upkeep go above your means to pay for it. You are generous and are especially generous when it comes to your children. You have been known to partake in gambling as a way of having fun.

Leo as a Saver

Your self-confidence and desire to succeed typically bring you success in earning money. You work hard to keep your head high above water and rise above the norm. You consequently may have a significant lump sum of savings or have the potential to accumulate a sizeable amount in your lifetime. You are intensely proud and do not want to ever appear in need of money. You need to fulfill your image of self-sufficiency and you know that means having sufficient savings to back your future endeavors.

Money Tips for Leo

- Looking successful can lead to success but beware of excesses when spending to achieve the look you are striving for.

- Lump sums of cash should be incorporated into a savings plan as soon as they are received.

- Beware of your pride as it can drive you to make poor money decisions. Take your ego out of the equation and think about your desired possessions with an objective point of view.

- You can be a great motivator to others to be financially successful.

- It is likely you already have a financial plan in place, but if not, consider having one prepared.

♍

VIRGO AND MONEY

Virgo as a Spender

With a Virgo personality, not only can you draw up a realistic budget but you can also stick to it.

If you wanted to, you could account for every purchase, right to the dime. You think nothing of digging into the details of cost and quality comparisons before you buy. As a discriminating buyer, you rarely regret the choices you make. Most of your purchases are practical and serve a useful purpose in your life. It is a rare event when you acquire something that is frivolous. You have a special interest in products that can improve your health as well as products that help you keep things organized and tidy. You need control over your possessions as you feel it is your responsibility for their upkeep. You are always eager to share your discovery of useful things with others, especially if you believe it will improve their wellbeing.

Virgo as a Saver

Given that you are a discriminating spender, you are correspondingly a disciplined and methodical saver. You have an appreciation for the need to have funds available in case of emergencies. You also understand the need for allocating money to save for special purchases, such as a home. You have no qualms about keeping up a saving routine if there is a meaningful purchase needed down the road. You have given attention to saving for retirement and it is likely, if you have focused on this, that you have a savings plan in place for funding older age.

Money Tips for Virgo

- Don't expect a perfect saving scenario to unfold; there are always unexpected spending needs.

- It is likely that you have already drawn up a comprehensive financial plan. If not, it is never too early to make one.

- Don't become discouraged if your detailed financial plan goes astray as you know only too well that everything will settle back into a logical order in due time with some calculated adjustments.

- Splurge on yourself once in awhile and indulge in being impractical.

Ω

LIBRA AND MONEY

Libra as a Spender

To buy or not to buy, that is the Libra question. It is sometimes difficult for you to make a decision on your own and you will likely get input from your partner and friends before you open your wallet. You take your time weighing all the pros and cons before you buy something. The last thing you want to be is disappointed with your purchase later on if it doesn't meet up to your high expectations or your partner's. You excel at perceiving intrinsic value and have a great eye for beauty. Your tastes in style and design are refined and you will spend accordingly to satisfy your senses as well as your partner's. You intuitively know how things should fit into your life and you avoid excesses in order to keep life stress-free and ascetically pleasing.

Libra as a Saver

You take a balanced approach to spending and saving. You will take time to make a plan and then reach your saving goals. Once you have decided on a way to save, you are committed to follow your plan. Money is a means for you to keep your life on an even keel and avoid hardship so you are concerned about having enough savings for your future needs. You are keen to engage your partner to save together.

Money Tips for Libra

- Don't be coerced into buying things that you don't really want.

- Trust your own intuition since others, as trusting as they may appear, can have their own agenda that is not in your best interest.

- For peace of mind, have a financial plan prepared.

- Conflicts can arise over money; avoid compromising at your own cost just to keep the peace.

♏

SCORPIO AND MONEY

Scorpio as a Spender

With a Scorpio personality, you have a very good handle on your wants and what needs to be done to fulfill them. You have a keen mind to dig deep and reveal good value for your money. You rarely overpay beyond what you believe something is worth. When you spend, you can do so on a large scale without hesitation. You are discreet with most of your possessions and prefer not to flaunt them. You recognize that money can be used in a way that can wield power behind the scenes to melt walls that keep you from getting what you want.

Scorpio as a Saver

You must be self-reliant and as a result, you are a diligent saver. You have high endurance and can work very hard to achieve success. You are drawn to work in a position that offers prestige and a high salary. You may have an intense drive to amass wealth and can deny yourself pleasures in order to stay on track. At the same time, it is difficult for you to suppress your feelings when you really want something and you will most likely dip into your savings to indulge.

Money Tips for Scorpio

- You should avoid making financial decisions at times when your emotional energy is high. Wait until the dust is settled and you see the situation in clearer terms.

- Keep things simple. Finance is more or less black and white and requires straightforward decisions; there is little need to waste energy trying to decode any hidden meanings.

- You are exceptional when it comes to getting down to the bottom of things; don't expect others to be at your speed or ability.

- It is likely that you already have a financial plan in place and have envisioned your future needs; otherwise, consider doing so.

SAGITTARIUS AND MONEY

Sagittarius as a Spender

Money is just a means to an end for the Sagittarian personality. You will spend freely without much consideration of cost. Possessions rarely possess you as your value system is drawn to intangibles such as the freedom to travel with little baggage. Your biggest expense is often the cost of travel or just going for frequent outings in town which you readily accept as the price of being able to uplift your spirits and provide yourself with adventure. You intuitively know what you want. You think fast and don't hesitate to open your wallet. If something is not within your reach, you find a way to be able to acquire it in short course.

Sagittarius as a Saver

Saving is not your forte as you often spend faster than what you earn. The upside is that you are always on the move looking for opportunities and you find employment quite readily. If an area of work provides you with sufficient stimulation and ability to intellectually grow, you may have a steady stream of income that can afford you an opportunity to save. You are not generally concerned about having enough money for your later years.

Money Tips for Sagittarius

- Face the fact; if you want to travel you are going to have to save for travel expenses.

- Do not fall prey to impulsive buying; take some time to consider the financial aftermath.

- Beware of being overly optimistic with your financial affairs as you could set yourself up for disillusionments and then disappointments.

- If you have a steady flow of income, set up an automatic savings plan that systematically transfers funds to your savings account.

- It is never too early to have a financial plan prepared to show you what amount of savings you are going to need, especially if you want to have an active lifestyle when older.

♑

CAPRICORN AND MONEY

Capricorn as a Spender

With a Capricorn personality, spending your money is a serious matter. You will explore all the options before committing funds to a purchase. You have strong reasoning ability and that bodes well for making good financial decisions. Once you made up your mind, you rarely change it. You respect and admire fine craftsmanship and appreciate the effort put into making quality goods. You are a loyal customer if your needs are met to your satisfaction, which is a high standard to achieve.

Capricorn as a Saver

Given that you are practical and disciplined, you are the type of saver that a financial planner would want as a model client. Security in life is a high priority with you and money can provide that sense of security you desire. Working hard is second nature to you and setting funds aside for your future money needs is doable and sensible. Until that time when your savings are slated for withdrawal, you are reluctant to touch them unless you are faced with dire financial circumstances.

Money Tips for Capricorn

- Bravo for being close to perfect when it comes to handling your money; don't expect others to be as diligent and be more accepting of their ways.

- Try tapping into your intuition when making financial choices; you will surprise yourself just how remarkable it can be in revealing an appropriate direction.

- You may have already created your own financial plan; if not, you would find having one prepared a satisfying experience

AQUARIUS AND MONEY

Aquarius as a Spender

One never knows what you are going to spend money on with an Aquarian personality. Your acquisitions can be novel and you may even surprise yourself. You like to socialize and take part in group activities and entertaining with friends makes up a good portion of how you like to spend your money. You are fond of buying the latest in technological devices and are eager to get your hands on new and improved models. You have the reputation of being a terrific fund-raiser for non-profit causes.

Aquarius as a Saver

Saving money often goes against your grain as you view it as rule-based and restricting. You do recognize that having money is necessary to bring some of your visions to fruition. You would rather achieve your wealth in unconventional ways and let it be a by-product of your ingenious efforts. You are patient and over time a portion of your remunerations do make their way into your savings.

Money Tips for Aquarius

- Set up an automatic savings plan that systematically transfers funds to your savings account and requires minimal attention on your part.

- Have a financial plan prepared to give you an appreciation of what you need to save for future needs.

- Solicit opinions from your close friends before you make any major purchases.

- You have an intellectual and societal viewpoint; accept that others may be more emotional with money issues and they make decisions on a more personal level.

♓

PISCES AND MONEY

Pisces as a Spender

With a Pisces personality, you are impressionable and can be easily influenced by others. By adopting other people's desires, you are prone to spending money for things that you may really not need. You have a plethora of books and music. Watching movies is something you cannot do without. You have a natural ability to understand what makes people tick and are a great observer of how other people spend their money. You are generous with friends and would give your last dollar to someone in need.

Pisces as a Saver

Accumulating money is rarely a goal for Pisces. Your longings are more esoteric and you have little interest in money aspirations. It is possible that someone can have an inspiring influence on you to save your money and you are capable of focusing and following through with a savings plan. You can easily feel overwhelmed with the responsibility of saving. Consequently, you prefer to pass that responsibility on to another.

Money Tips for Pisces

- Have an automatic savings plan set up that can provide you with a path of least resistance to save for your future needs.

- A financial plan that formalizes what has to be done to put your finances in order would give you a clear action plan.

- Your creative imagination can be tapped into to dream up great money saving ideas; (one can only dream that this could happen).

- Beware of people trying to delude you into buying things you don't really need.

CHAPTER 3

INVESTING

A BALANCED APPROACH

Often when you are excited about making an investment that you *feel* sure will bring about a great return, you want to invest a relatively large amount of your money to buy it. Holding a one-investment bet that takes up a good share of the value of your investment portfolio could pay off in a big way, but it could also devastate your wealth if things don't work out. The bottom line is that this way of extreme investing is not worth the risk and it would be regrettable to learn that lesson the hard way. This is especially true when you are retired and have no employment means to recoup your losses.

A well designed and balanced portfolio is what is needed to have peace of mind and ride out all the volatility that comes with fast moving global money flows. This includes making sure you have suitable diversification in asset classes such as bonds and equities as well as a well thought out mix of holdings within those asset classes.

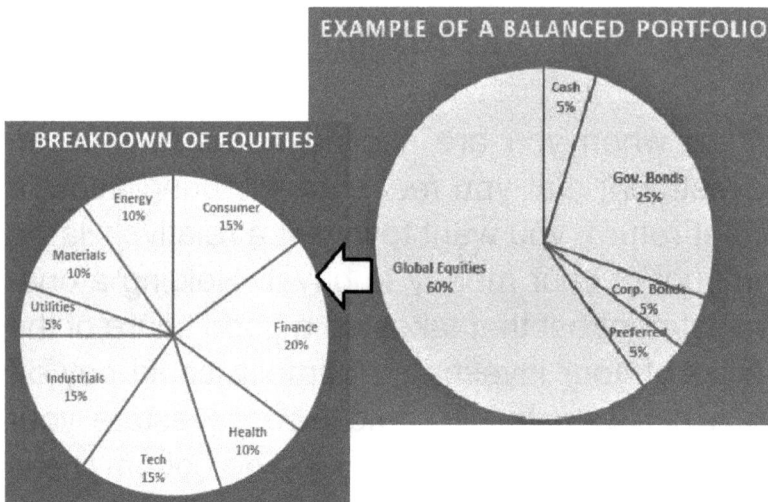

EXAMPLE OF A BALANCED PORTFOLIO

BREAKDOWN OF EQUITIES

Energy 10%
Consumer 15%
Materials 10%
Utilities 5%
Finance 20%
Industrials 15%
Tech 15%
Health 10%

Cash 5%
Gov. Bonds 25%
Global Equities 60%
Corp. Bonds 5%
Preferred 5%

Individual investors are becoming more attuned to having *globally diverse portfolios* with investment holdings that are outside of their home country. Other countries can provide greater growth opportunities but each country comes with its own unique risks, such as currency and political risks. These additional risks have to be taken into account.

MARKET VOLATILITY

"The only function of economic forecasting is to make astrology look respectable."
John Kenneth Galbraith

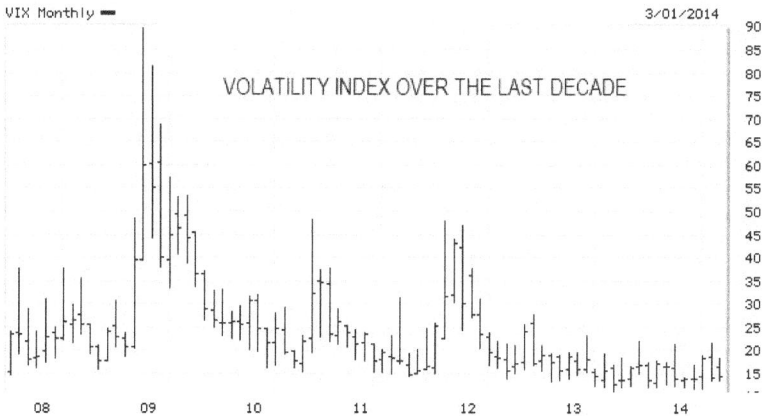

VIX Monthly ▬   3/01/2014

VOLATILITY INDEX OVER THE LAST DECADE

```
90
85
80
75
70
65
60
55
50
45
40
35
30
25
20
15
```

08   09   10   11   12   13   14

Have you ever been on the bank of a river upstream from a roaring waterfall and made note of how peaceful the river looked before it innocently plunged over the cliff. Investment markets can lull you into thinking they will continue to flow smoothly along. Sooner or later though, there will be waterfalls. Alas, it is emotionally trying to live through market turbulences. Patience is a strong investor virtue. Fortunately, extreme volatility in the markets is normally short-lived as can be seen in the chart above showing the volatility of Standard and Poor's 500 Index (VIX) (a broad measure of the volatility of the US stock market).

INVESTING WAYS

Nowadays, technology allows you to easily invest at low cost on your own using an on-line investment account. An abundance of research information is accessible over the internet for you to be able to identify and analyze potential investments.

For those individuals who prefer not to have the responsibility of managing their own portfolios, financial advisors are readily available to handle the task. The cost of advisory services is an important consideration as it can erode your wealth significantly over time.

Given the increasing demand for management of retirement savings by the retiring baby boomers, competition in the financial service industry is bringing down the cost of financial advice. On-line investment management services that provide *automatic rebalancing* of portfolios' asset allocations are becoming more numerous with very low management fees.

THE DIFFERENT INVESTOR MINDSETS

Below are descriptions of the different Zodiac investors followed by investment advice that will provide insights into how to make wise investment decisions.

♈

ARIES AND INVESTING

Aries as an Investor

You are attracted to whatever is hot in the stock market. You do not have much interest in investing in bonds or interest-bearing types of deposits. You enjoy picking winners in the battle for corporate survival. Any losers you end up with are quickly dismissed and forgotten.

Investment Advice to Aries

There is no point to tell you to stop and think about your money decisions before acting, because this just isn't going to happen. For major financial decisions, you must have a partner that you trust to assist you. This can be a professional financial advisor or someone who knows you well, has your best interests at heart, and has financial expertise. You have to appreciate that you are too impulsive when making these types of important decisions. A balanced approach to investing with a portfolio holding both stocks and bonds will make you a winner in the long run.

℧

TAURUS AND INVESTING

Taurus as an Investor

You are a cautious investor. Risk is a very ugly word to you. You would prefer your portfolio to have minimal exposure to the ups and downs of the stock market. It is difficult for you to conceive of investing outside your home country. Most of your money is in so-called 'safe' investments and you want to preserve it. You are impressed with financial advisors who have been in the business for a long time, have been through the trials of investing and speak in a cautionary tone.

Investment Advice to Taurus

Even the investments labelled as 'safe' can have a risk associated with them. Interest-paying investments, such as government bonds, are subject to price declines when interest rates rise. Preserving wealth means hedging against risks such as inflation as well as the opportunity cost of not having any growth exposure in your portfolio. Being able to capture growth in expanding economic sectors in different areas of the world would contribute to preserving your wealth during the times your home economy is stagnant. It would be prudent to have a balanced approach to investing and that means having a portfolio that includes a conservative mix of bonds along with a diversified mix of global stocks. Review your existing portfolio with this advice in mind and adjust it accordingly either by yourself or with the aid of a financial advisor that you trust implicitly.

II

GEMINI AND INVESTING

Gemini as an Investor

Based on your readings and talking with others, you can generate many smart ideas that can be translated into money-making investments, so many in fact that it can be difficult for you to select. As time flies by, you have probably only acted on a few, or perhaps none, of your ideas. In the meantime, your money is sitting in cash making minimal interest.

Investment Advice to Gemini

It is time to focus on an investment plan if you have not yet done so. Set aside time and devote yourself solely to accomplishing this task. Use a balanced approach in building a diversified portfolio that includes both stocks and bonds. It may be prudent to avoid buying individual stocks if you find the universe of potential candidates unwieldy. Consider instead large exchange-traded-fund indices to keep your search more simplified. If you prefer to use a financial advisor, use someone who is up to your speed of thought that you can communicate well with. Your friends can provide referrals.

CANCER AND INVESTING

Cancer as an Investor

You do recognize you need to have an investment plan to provide for a comfortable life. You are able to perceive business opportunities and have a good sense of timing that can contribute to making profitable investments. Specific ways of how to manage your savings are not of much interest to you and you generally prefer to leave that up to a financial advisor. You have strong negative emotions when you lose money. You instinctively have an urge to sell all investments that are dipping in value when the markets get volatile. Your financial advisor should be aware of your wariness when investing your savings and be able to ease your concerns and keep you on a steady course when the markets are rocky.

Investment Advice to Cancer

It is guaranteed that the markets will test your emotions and make you explode probably more than once in your lifetime. A seasoned financial advisor has experienced these market turbulences and should help you make a portfolio that can weather most difficult markets. It is this type of investing support you, as a Cancer personality, should seek. A family member may be able to refer you to such a trustworthy individual.

♌

LEO AND INVESTING

Leo as an Investor

You are capable of being the captain at the helm of your investment portfolio if you so desire. You are forward thinking and can make sound investment decisions. Your strong convictions can sometimes entice you to make large bets and if successful, can lead you to make even larger bets. It takes one significant investment loss to make you wary of risk. You then learn how to be a more prudent investor and avoid excessive risk.

Investment Advice to Leo

Learn as much as you can about investing for you have the makeup to be very successful at it. Swallow your pride if you make a bad investment choice and learn from where you may have miscalculated risk. You tend to underestimate risk as you have a very positive outlook. Keep your investment decisions to yourself as then your personal pride will not come into play and you will keep a clear and logical mind. If you consult with a financial advisor, that person's role will be to provide you with information that you don't already have and assist you in carrying out your decisions.

VIRGO AND INVESTING

Virgo as an Investor

It is sometimes difficult for you to see the investment forest for the trees. You can be very knowledgeable on a specific way to invest and may not have considered the need for any other way. Your investment portfolio can often be skewed in one asset type, for example, just blue chip stocks that pay dividends. You are a measured risk taker and it is unlikely you would make a large bet on one particular investment

Investment Advice to Virgo

Review your investment portfolio and study its balance relative to the weightings of stocks and bonds. As well, examine the diversity of the stocks and the maturities of the bonds. You may find a predominance of an investment type in your portfolio. For example, you may have a large sum in one bond maturing 20 years down the road. Even though this investment itself may be considered low risk, it is risky to have a portfolio overweight in one type of investment. There are many resources that you tap into to expand your knowledge of investing and develop a well balanced, diversified portfolio. You have the mind to be able to research and accomplish this. It would be difficult for you to delegate the task of investing to another, but a financial advisor who works with you as a team player could open your eyes to alternatives you never had come close to considering. Keep in mind there is no perfect investment portfolio as there are too many unknown future events that can affect it.

♎

LIBRA AND INVESTING

Libra as an Investor

Words of investment advice from trusting individuals are meaningful to you and you often defer to their judgment even if it differs from your thoughts. You prefer to have someone else take care of your investment portfolio as investing is not really of interest to you and can be unsettling. That is not to say that you are not a keen observer of worldly events that affect the investment markets, especially political events.

Investment Advice to Libra

The need for a balanced portfolio that is well diversified to hedge risk is something that you can easily appreciate. Your dislike of volatility and unsettling investment markets makes it advisable to have your portfolio managed by a professional. Partner up with one who has a pleasant temperament to your liking and who can eloquently explain investment strategies. Review your portfolio with your advisor on an annual basis and in the meantime, avoid get perturbed over market fluctuations

♏

SCORPIO AND INVESTING

Scorpio as an Investor

You have a deep mind that can hold many details and like an elephant, you never forget. This affords you the ability to remember your investment winners and losers and what investment criteria you should and should not repeat. You have little time or tolerance for those who promote investments that sound too good to be true. They are worthy of your wrath. You may not feel that managing your own investments is a productive use of your time as you may prefer to be directing your energies towards deeper pursuits.

Investment Advice to Scorpio

Hire an investment advisor that meets your standards of clarity and strength of character. This person should have strong analytical skills and a thorough knowledge of how to assess investment risk. As well, this person will have to be able to handle your intensity and directness. If things do not progress to your liking, move on and get on with another approach. Burning bridges are a waste of your precious energy and can work against you.

SAGITTARIUS AND INVESTING

Sagittarius as an Investor

You can identify investment opportunities long before the crowd. You intuitively grasp the potential for new ideas. You have a global perspective and can identify growth prospects in many regions of the world. If you believe in capitalism and you recognize its value, you have the ability to be very successful in investing in innovative companies. It is probable though that you have little interest in the subject of investing. You can be impulsive when making investment choices and you may lack the patience required to do research.

Investment Advice for Sagittarius

It is advisable that you work with a financial advisor to manage your investment portfolio. You need an advisor who is frank and upfront with you as this is your style of communicating. It would be beneficial to share your positive and forward outlook with your advisor. Bear with the markets when they are on downtrends and don't make any rash decisions during this time. Rely on your advisor's advice to keep your portfolio balanced. A long term financial plan would be worthwhile to have. If you inherit any lump sums, don't hesitate to get financial advice.

♑

CAPRICORN AND INVESTING

Capricorn as an Investor

You are a conservative investor. You are opposed to being subjected to volatile returns in your investment portfolio. You accept the consequences of major market downturns but become wary of endangering your investments to the possibility of that happening again. You like to be in control of your investments and like to make your own investment decisions. You have a financial goal in sight and are determined to reach it.

Investment Advice for Capricorn

The more experience you gain in investing and surviving the dramatic market swings that are inevitable, the better you become at tolerating risk. You eventually will recognize that a balanced approach to investing does hedge risk and reduce volatility. As you become more seasoned at investing, you can go outside your former risk boundaries and consider investments that have greater potential for growth and at the same time add more diversification to your portfolio. Think globally when you invest; the world is your oyster to reap investment returns.

AQUARIUS AND INVESTING

Aquarius as an Investor

You are very oriented towards thinking about the future. Given you like to follow advancements in technology, you are drawn to investments in the technology sector. You may approach investing as a way to influence societal values such as through specialty funds that focus on 'ethical' investing. You like to share investing ideas with people who are on the same mental plane as yourself and you may find yourself involved in an investment club.

Investment Advice for Aquarius

Investing in potential growth opportunities play a role but should not be the entire focus of an investment portfolio. Investments in income-generating holdings, such as proven companies that have a history of paying dividends, can provide income, diversification and reduce risk in the overall portfolio. Review your investment portfolio and see if it balanced sufficiently with fixed income and equities. Tap into your capacity of being able to have a broad vision, and take a global approach when investing.

♓

PISCES AND INVESTING

Pisces as an Investor

You are more likely to be spending your time taking care of others rather than paying attention to your own investments. The emotional drag of the ups and downs of investment markets does not bode well for your peace of mind. You may have opened several investment accounts over the years that you may have lost track of.

Investment Advice for Pisces

Consolidate all of your investment accounts if you have more than one. Work with one financial advisor who you have been referred to by at least two trustworthy friends. In addition to your financial advisor, have another trusting individual (who has never requested money from you) review your portfolio with you on an annual basis.   If you inherit any lump sums, don't hesitate to get financial advice as per the above referral process.   Avoid being swayed by your emotions to give funds to those in need who in reality have the ability to help themselves.

CHAPTER 4

MONEY RELATIONSHIPS

FINANCIAL PLANNING

"Expect the best, plan for the worst, and prepare to be surprised."
Dennis Waitley

All types of money relationships between two individuals call for some degree of 'financial planning' where the big picture is looked at to determine future financial spending needs and priorities of the parties involved. In addition, other complexities that can have significant monetary impacts such as children's needs, estate planning, life insurance considerations, pensions, and taxation issues can also come into play when preparing a financial plan.

Keep in mind that a financial plan is just a 'plan'; it takes energy and determination to carry it through to the realization of goals. It can also be subject to revisions as many unknowns can arise that alter the financial formulas. For example, the resulting rate of investment return can be significantly different than what was originally programmed in the financial plan. An objective, professional Financial Planner can help in the process of making a financial plan, *especially when the parties involved have different money mindsets.*

HARMONIOUS MONEY RELATIONSHIPS

Financial harmony abounds when two Zodiac Signs have similar money viewpoints and habits that lead to positive results. The two can blend their efforts in a cooperative fashion and have great synergy. Financial decisions can come easily and both support each others desires for possessions and spending habits. The sharing of money feels fair and equitable. This does not mean that there is a certainty for wealth. Some harmonious relationships strive more than others to reach their financial goals.

COMPENSATING MONEY RELATIONSHIPS

The strengths of one Zodiac Sign can compensate for the weaknesses of the other and vice-versa. Together, the Signs mesh in a virtuous balance and they can make financial decisions in an agreeable manner that satisfies both parties.

ONE-SIDED MONEY RELATIONSHIPS

Some Zodiac Signs are more powerful than others. These forceful signs dominate in the relationship. So, whatever that stronger money personality is, that will be the nature of the combined money habits most of the time. The suppressed individual can have an emotional outburst and rebel when the situation is no longer tolerable. On the other hand, some Zodiac signs are happy to shrug off money responsibilities and have someone else handle all of the finances.

OPPOSING MONEY RELATIONSHIPS

When two Zodiac Signs have opposing money personalities, conflicts can arise and it is difficult to reach compromises and commit to a joint financial plan. A solution can be for each party to go their separate ways when it comes to financing their personal spending habits, have their own savings and investment accounts, and go 50/50 on common overhead expenses.

THE ZODIAC MONEY RELATIONSHIPS

Below are descriptions of the different Zodiac money relationships between two Signs that can be one of the following: harmonious, compensating, one-sided or opposing. These relationships obviously exist between two individuals, but they also can reside *within* one individual. For example, if an individual has Virgo and Pisces' archetypes influencing his/her money decisions, this can cause tension and difficulty in making personal financial decisions for reasons you can read below.

♈

ARIES' MONEY RELATIONSHIPS

Aries' Viewpoint: *"Money is a means to get what I need right now and get on with my life."*

Aries and Aries

This can often be an *opposing money relationship* since both parties want their own way and want to be the first to claim it. Both are self-centered and their own personal needs come first. This can also be a *harmonious money relationship* if you both have the same financial desires and personal wants since your drives are tremendous and, no doubt, you can get whatever you aim for with your combined efforts.

Aries and Taurus

As a *compensating money relationship*, Aries is just the person that Taurus needs to 'go for it' and secure their financial goals. Taurus will pin Aries down, relay the premeditated money mission to Aries, say that it was Aries' idea to begin with and then point Aries' head in the proper direction of action. Aries happily doesn't have to think about anything else except charging ahead, staying o n course and be the first to claim victory. In the meantime, Taurus can lean back and indulge in sensual pleasures.

Aries and Gemini

As a *compensating money relationship*, Gemini can generate the most clever money ideas but is not so keen to take the time to see any of them to fruition. Aries can seize one of these ideas, and put their finances into direct action. Both can lose sight of what the original idea was if Gemini sidetracks Aries and Aries starts on a new course of action.

Aries and Cancer

This is generally an *opposing money relationship* as Cancer feels that Aries is far too impulsive with money issues. This makes Cancer feel insecure and this takes its toll on Cancer's emotions. Aries thinks Cancer is too sensitive and moody over money issues and doesn't hesitate to inform Cancer of this. Cancer deeply resents this brusqueness and finds it difficult to shrug it off.

Aries and Leo

This can be a *harmonious money relationship,* a dynamite duo especially if Aries lets Leo be publicly recognized as the one who is responsible for their financial successes. Leo has no problem letting Aries carry out their financial plans, as long as Aries doesn't dishonor Leo in any way. Aries has to accept Leo's need for a prestigious image. Leo will have to humor Aries' need for personal impulsive desires.

Aries and Virgo

This can be a *compensating money relationship* given Virgo can tolerate Aries' impulsive spending behavior. Virgo does admire Aries' great energy drive to try and accomplish their financial goals. Aries admires Virgo's incredible mind for drawing up the detailed plans. But this can also work against Virgo if Aries finds Virgo just too nitpicky with the details, accounting for every dollar. As these personalities become more entrenched in their ways, this could result in an *opposing money relationship*.

Aries and Libra

This can be a *one-sided money relationship*, as Aries can be too self-assertive and forceful for Libra to be able to express money concerns.
Libra will gladly rely on Aries to carry out their financial goals and will keep the peace by letting Aries pursue the chase without putting up any roadblocks.

Aries and Scorpio

This could work as a *compensating money relationship* if Scorpio feels comfortable in relinquishing some control when carrying out their financial plans. Scorpio recognizes Aries' high energy drive and potential. Scorpio will try to keep Aries under rein and Aries may lambaste Scorpio for trying to do so. Aries blunt words could be just too cutting for Scorpio's feelings, ending up in an *opposing money relationship*. Butting heads could have regrettable consequences, especially for Aries in the long run.

Aries and Sagittarius

This can be a *harmonious money relationship* as long as the parties' financial goals are in sync. Aries will have to keep the "I wants" at bay and Sagittarius will have to keep a limit on the number of outings to "broaden our outlook on life" if both are to keep the peace on how their money is spent. There is enough energy to spare in this relationship to put towards reaching a financial goal if they can focus on this mission.

This is easier said than done since both parties are often preoccupied with pursuing other multiple goals.

Aries and Capricorn

This can be a *compensating money relationship* if Capricorn can appreciate the energy drive of Aries to achieve financial goals. Aries can take advantage of Capricorn's disciplined logic and preparation of a long-term road map for financial success. It is Capricorn that just may not be able to handle Aries' impulsive spending habits if they get too out of hand. In that case, an *opposing money relationship* can arise.

Aries and Aquarius

This can be an *opposing money relationship* as both parties are strongly independent and love their freedom and that includes freedom to handle their money the way they see fit. Aquarius may find it difficult to accept Aries' self-centeredness and Aries may find Aquarius' wants eccentric and frustrating to achieve as they are often far-fetched.

Aries and Pisces

This is a *one-sided money relationship* where the forceful Aries calls the shots on the finances. Pisces has little desire to rock the boat and will yield to Aries. Pisces inspires Aries and can share imaginative dreams that Aries can make 'come true'.

ö

TAURUS' MONEY RELATIONSHIPS

Taurus' Viewpoint: *"Money enables me to fulfill my need for possessions that enrich my life."*

Taurus and Aries

This can be a *compensating money relationship*. See *'Aries and Taurus'* described above.

Taurus and Taurus

This is a generally *harmonious money relationship*, where both parties have a deep need for financial security. There may be some discord as to who is going to take the initiative to put the financial plans into action. Both are able to wait patiently to savor the pleasures of their financial rewards.

Taurus and Gemini

This can be a *compensating money* relationship as Taurus does recognize how witty Gemini can be with financial affairs. Gemini gains a comforting sense of financial stability from predictable Taurus. Taurus can be a procrastinator and Gemini can have a short attention span, so putting financial plans into action can be problematic.

Taurus and Cancer

This can be a *harmonious money relationship* as both parties value being financially secure and will commit to working together to attain this security. Both Taurus and Cancer like stability and resist change so neither will pull any financial surprises on the other. Predictable money habits make their lives comfortable together.

Taurus and Leo

This can be a *harmonious money relationship*. Both enjoy luxuries and the good things in life. Leo knows that work is required to accumulate wealth and Taurus appreciates the practicalities that are necessary to reach financial goals. Taurus learns how to compliment Leo on financial prowess and Leo revels in Taurus' delight of beautiful possessions. Taurus needs to be able to tolerate letting Leo be generous with their possessions as Leo likes to share them with others.

Taurus and Virgo

This is a *harmonious money relationship*. Taurus can direct the big financial picture and Virgo can handle all the details perfectly. They work well together as they patiently accumulate wealth, both desiring financial security.

Taurus and Libra

This is a *one-sided money relationship* with Taurus as the leader in making financial decisions. Libra is happy to have Taurus handle the finances and be in charge of the purchases that beautify and decorate their lives.

Taurus and Scorpio

This can be a *harmonious money relationship* only if they can open up and share their financial secret desires with each other (which is easier said than done). Scorpio seeks the deep emotional peace that financial security can impart. Taurus knows only too well that having money means indulging in comforts. If both are willing, Taurus and Scorpio can strategize brilliantly together to achieve financial success.

Taurus and Sagittarius

This can be a *compensating financial relationship* if Taurus is willing to adopt some of Sagittarius' riskier financial ideas that counterpoise Taurus' conservative stance, resulting in a better balance. Both parties will reap the additional monetary rewards that come with calculated risk-taking over time.

Taurus and Capricorn

This is a *harmonious money relationship*. Capricorn can realistically assess the money situation and is capable of superior financial planning. Taurus will support the routine that the financial plan calls for. Both are conservative and patient. Both highly value the home and possessions; Capricorn tends to view them as investments more so than Taurus who views them as sources of comfort and pleasure.

Taurus and Aquarius

This is a *one-sided money relationship* with Taurus making the majority of the financial decisions and setting the tone for spending and saving. Aquarius will accept what the financial expectations are in order to avoid having to deal with the onerous responsibility of Taurus' financial desires.

Taurus and Pisces

This is a *one-sided money relationship* with Taurus making all of the financial decisions. Pisces has little interest in money matters. Pisces instinctively knows that Taurus is more capable of financial planning and prefers to avoid the emotional impact of money matters.

Ⅱ

GEMINI'S MONEY RELATIONSHIPS

Gemini's Viewpoint: *"Money enables me to partake in mentally stimulating pursuits to make my life interesting and varied."*

Gemini and Aries

This can be a *compensating money relationship.* See *'Aries and Gemini'* described above.

Gemini and Taurus

This can be a *compensating money relationship.* See *'Taurus and Gemini'* described above.

Gemini and Gemini

This is a *harmonious money relationship* and they will talk openly and share their findings on how to financially plan. They both will gobble up information from people and a variety of sources on personal finance. Who will take the first step in executing the financial plan is another issue as neither party really wants to commit to this given it is much more fun talking about doing it.

Gemini and Cancer

This is a *compensating money relationship* where Cancer pieces together the money aspirations and has the final say in how the financial plan comes together. Gemini will uncover a number of perceptive options for Cancer to consider.

Gemini and Leo

This is a *compensating money relationship* where Leo is suitably impressed with Gemini's gift of intelligence for money ideas. Leo inspires Gemini to acquire financial knowledge and Gemini feels like an important contributor to their financial well-being by sharing ideas with Leo. Gemini is pleased to have Leo execute the financial plans.

Gemini and Virgo

This can be a *one-sided money relationship* and Virgo will be in control of the finances. Virgo just doesn't want to risk having a financial plan go astray. Gemini relinquishes control happily as Gemini knows just how great Virgo can organize and carry out their financial plans. Gemini would rather not ignite Virgo's criticism of not being focused when the task of money management is being called for.

Gemini and Libra

This is a *harmonious money relationship*. Gemini respects Libra's ability to fairly compromise with any of their differing money desires. Libra admires Gemini's intellectual reasoning powers. Neither are particularly fond of buckling down and putting a financial plan into action even though they both agree it should be done.

Gemini and Scorpio

This can be a *one-sided financial relationship* with Scorpio single-handedly making financial commitments for both parties. Gemini has learned to trust that Scorpio will act in their best interests and generally the finances are in good shape. Gemini recognizes that Scorpio needs to be in control of the money moves.

Gemini and Sagittarius

This can be a *harmonious money relationship*. Both Gemini and Sagittarius will intellectualize their money desires and rationalize their financial plans. Gemini will come up with creative money ideas and Sagittarius will often just want to "let's see and try it". Neither really want to deal with money obstacles that are inevitable and financial planning can quickly go astray.

Gemini and Capricorn

This is a *one-sided money relationship* and Capricorn will be in charge. Capricorn will independently draw up a thorough financial plan and will be determined to see it through. Gemini can research current money trends and relay this information to Capricorn to help in Capricorn's decision making.

Gemini and Aquarius

This can be a *harmonious money relationship.* Gemini is happy to discuss money topics with Aquarius and Aquarius will listen intently, admiring Gemini's ability to keep up with current issues. It is unlikely that either party is keen on binding themselves to a financial plan. Both parties are accepting of each others independent spending habits and their common spending is usually for social outings that they both enjoy indulging in.

Gemini and Pisces

This can be a *one-sided money relationship* where Gemini addresses the majority of financial issues.   Pisces is generally content with Gemini's quick wit to make money decisions. Pisces is happy to pass on these challenges and avoid experiencing any self-doubt on making the right money moves.

CANCER'S MONEY RELATIONSHIPS

Cancer's Viewpoint: *"Money provides me with a deep sense of security that I need."*

Cancer and Aries

This is generally an *opposing money relationship.* See *'Aries and Cancer'* described above.

Cancer and Taurus

This can be a *harmonious money relationship.* See *'Taurus and Cancer'* described above.

Cancer and Gemini

This is a *compensating money relationship.* See *'Gemini and Cancer'* described above.

Cancer and Cancer

This is a *harmonious money relationship.* Both parties have similar money priorities and desire material security. Both want to be emotionally reassured that they are on the right financial track and can sense what the other needs to have this peace of mind.

Cancer and Leo

This can be a *compensating money relationship* and a very successful one where Leo's forte to carry out their financial plans is tempered by Cancer's conservative money stance. This can result in a well-balanced approach to handling money.

Cancer and Virgo

This is a *compensating money relationship* and can result in a balanced approach to their financial plans. Virgo's logical and discriminating money mind complements Cancer's sensitivity to perceive and avoid risk. As long as Virgo can tolerate Cancer's mood swings with the ebb and flow of their finances and that Cancer can tolerate Virgo's critical analysis of their money situation, all will go well.

Cancer and Libra

This can be a *harmonious money relationship* where both parties want to please each other and avoid financial disagreements. Libra is a connoisseur of knowing what Cancer needs to hear to make Cancer feel secure about money decisions. Cancer adheres to conservative financial planning that assures Libra of financial stability.

Cancer and Scorpio

This is a *harmonious money relationship* where a solid money foundation can assure success with their financial plans. Scorpio will be the emotional rock of strength when financial difficulties arise. Cancer will patiently and methodically build on their financial goals. The two appreciate each others solidarity to the financial plan.

Cancer and Sagittarius

This is an *opposing money relationship*. Sagittarius is outgoing, is not concerned about long-term financial goals and prefers to individually handle money. Cancer values stability and needs a large dose of financial security that Sagittarius is not willing to commit to striving for. Cancer can get upset over

Sagittarius' adventurous spending habits. Sagittarius will be acutely frank in telling Cancer to stay clear.

Cancer and Capricorn

This can be a *harmonious money relationship.* Cancer recognizes Capricorn's strong will to lead the way and achieve their financial goals. Cancer enjoys the sense of stability that Capricorn emanates. Capricorn appreciates Cancer's conservative money logic and emotional support. Both can take their time to determine a solid financial plan but once it is decided on, they are determined to move forward on solid footing.

Cancer and Aquarius

This is an *opposing money relationship.* Cancer's need for financial assurance cannot be fulfilled by Aquarius. Aquarius does not want to be tied down by financial goals and needs freedom and independence with money matters.

Cancer finds Aquarius' indifference to their financial issues emotionally disturbing and their money values dissimilar.

Cancer and Pisces

This is a *one-sided money relationship* where Cancer takes the leading role with the finances. Pisces is happy to pass this role onto Cancer and Pisces fully trusts that Cancer will have their well-being in mind when handling their money. Cancer will assume the responsibilities with a conservative and practical approach. Pisces fully understands Cancer's need for financial security.

♌

LEO'S MONEY RELATIONSHIPS

Leo's Viewpoint: *"Money makes me feel dignified and allows me to be generous to others."*

Leo and Aries

This can be a *harmonious money relationship.* See *'Aries and Leo'* described above.

Leo and Taurus

This can be a *harmonious money relationship.* See *'Taurus and Leo'* described above.

Leo and Gemini

This is a *compensating money relationship.* See *'Gemini and Leo'* described above.

Leo and Cancer

This can be a *compensating money relationship.* See *'Cancer and Leo'* described above.

Leo and Leo

This can be a *harmonious money relationship,* or, could go the other way and be *an opposing money relationship.* Both Leos want to lead. If they have mutually benefitting financial objectives and take turns in taking the lead role when making money decisions, then these Leos will make a hyper-powerful money team. In opposition, the two Leos may arrogantly battle for domination and their pride can get in their way. Best to handle their own individual finances if opposition is the most common scenario.

Leo and Virgo

This is a *compensating money relationship.* Both Leo and Virgo are committed to seeing a financial plan through. Leo has great drive to get the ball rolling and Virgo will work behind the scenes diligently researching the best money moves. Leo brings much-needed fun to the money equation for Virgo when spending and respects Virgo's amazing mind for details. Virgo admires Leo's dignity and a mutual need for sophistication.

Leo and Libra

This is a *one-sided money relationship* where Leo is in charge of making the major financial decisions. Libra is content to take more of a minor role and will be flexible to adapt to Leo's financial plans. Both parties enjoy socializing and outings which take up a good chunk of their spending habits. Both will elegantly show off their possessions to stand out from the crowd.

Leo and Scorpio

This is an *opposing money relationship*. Both Leo and Scorpio will try and dominate each other with major money issues. Leo will be upfront in trying to lead and Scorpio will be underhanded with money handling. That can only bring about emotional friction. Leo will be infuriated to be subjugated. Scorpio eyes Leo's vanity and generosity to others as unnecessary expenses.

Leo and Sagittarius

This is a *harmonious money relationship* with both parties having similar money priorities. Both respect each others generous qualities. Leo has a more serious attitude towards money but Sagittarius takes this in stride and the two compromise easily. Leo appreciates Sagittarius' positive attitude when experiencing money difficulties.

Leo and Capricorn

This can be an *opposing money relationship*. It is unlikely that Capricorn will approve of Leo's spending desires and Capricorn will find Leo too extravagant. Leo will not want to be subjected to Capricorn's stringent discipline to sacrifice today's desires for tomorrow's needs. The two are strong-minded, so money compromises do not come easily. Best to have these two manage their finances independently.

Leo and Aquarius

This is a *compensating money relationship* where Leo takes the reins on carrying out money decisions and Aquarius contributes novel ways to help form those decisions. Leo admires Aquarius' intellect and individuality and Aquarius admires Leo's generosity and vitality.

Leo and Pisces

This is a *one-sided money relationship* where the money decisions are left entirely up to Leo. Pisces gladly leaves the financial affairs in Leo's court and is eternally grateful and compliments Leo for the initiative. Leo is confident to handle their financial plans solely and to be able to spend freely to keep up appearances.

♍

VIRGO'S MONEY RELATIONSHIPS

Virgo's Viewpoint: *"Money gives me the means to improve myself and live my life without being a burden to others."*

Virgo and Aries

This can be a *compensating money relationship.* See *'Aries and Virgo'* described above.

Virgo and Taurus

This is a *harmonious money relationship.* See *'Taurus and Virgo'* described above.

Virgo and Gemini

This can be a *one-sided money relationship.* See *'Gemini and Virgo'* described above.

Virgo and Cancer

This is a *compensating money relationship.* See *'Cancer and Virgo'* described above.

Virgo and Leo

This is a *compensating money relationship.* See *'Leo and Virgo'* described above.

Virgo and Virgo

This is a *harmonious money relationship.* Both parties have a practical approach to handling their finances. They are open with each other and consistently communicate where they stand with their money affairs. They generally have similar material goals and given this, their sharp, critical opinions are kept at bay. It is rare that they do not achieve their realistic financial goals.

Virgo and Libra

This is a *compensating money relationship*. Virgo takes pleasure in closely monitoring their finances and Libra takes pleasure in finding mutually enjoyable ways to spend their money. Both are forthright in communicating when there are money issues. Libra is talented at finding equitable compromises when needed.

Virgo and Scorpio

This is a *one-sided money relationship* and Scorpio wants to take charge of their finances and deliver their financial goals. Virgo allows Scorpio to do so and will readily contribute to Scorpio's ability to make good money decisions by researching the necessary details. Scorpio admires Virgo thoroughness when contributing and committing to a financial plan.

Virgo and Sagittarius

This is an *opposing money relationship.* Virgo finds Sagittarius too impetuous with spending their money and Virgo wants to keep their finances separate. Virgo endeavors to have a precise financial plan in place and followed and Sagittarius has no desire to commit to that financial plan on Virgo's exact terms. Sagittarius needs to be free to spend at will.

Virgo and Capricorn

This is a *harmonious money relationship.* Both parties will commit to working hard towards their financial goals. Capricorn needs to have a plan in place for a financially secure future and Virgo is completely onside. Together, they can realistically strategize ways for material success.

Virgo and Aquarius

This can be an *opposing money relationship.* Virgo finds Aquarius' lack of personal money goals and inconsistent spending habits frustrating. Aquarius finds Virgo's need to account for every dollar spent a waste of time. Virgo wants to focus on the nitty-gritty of how to achieve personal financial goals and plan ahead. Aquarius knows only too well how plans can go astray and would much rather deal with money issues only when they arise.

Virgo and Pisces

This can be an *opposing money relationship.* Virgo finds Pisces' way of approaching the subject of money as being too abstract and difficult to rationalize. Virgo is a realist and Pisces is a dreamer when it comes to financial goals. It is unlikely that Pisces can commit to a detailed financial plan that Virgo would expect to be adhered to.

Ω
___

LIBRA'S MONEY RELATIONSHIPS

Libra's Viewpoint: *"Money enables me keep my life in balance and to live with others harmoniously."*

Libra and Aries

This can be a *one-sided money relationship.* See *'Aries and Libra'* described above.

Libra and Taurus

This is a *one-sided money relationship.* See *'Taurus and Libra'* described above.

Libra and Gemini

This is a *harmonious money relationship.* See *'Gemini and Libra'* described above.

Libra and Cancer
This can be a *harmonious money relationship.*
See *'Cancer and Libra'* described above.

Libra and Leo

This is a *one-sided money relationship.* See
'Leo and Libra' described above.

Libra and Virgo

This is a *compensating money relationship.* See
'Virgo and Libra' described above.

Libra and Libra

This is a *harmonious money relationship.* Both
parties want to keep the peace and always have
the other in mind when they make financial
decisions. As long as they can focus and think
their financial goals through, they have a good
chance of succeeding. Libra can be easily side-
tracked and complacent about financial issues.

Libra and Scorpio

This is a *one-sided money relationship* with Scorpio making the financial decisions. Scorpio needs to be in control of the financial plan. Libra trusts Scorpio to be in charge although at times Scorpio can be secretive about money activities, keeping Libra in the dark. Libra likes to have Scorpio feel like the protector over their financial well-being and will provide ample compliments to boost Scorpio's confidence.

Libra and Sagittarius

This is a *one-sided money relationship* with Sagittarius handling the majority of the financial issues. Libra admires the directness of Sagittarius to quickly come to a financial decision, unlike Libra who takes a much longer time to weigh all the pros and cons. Both have similar desires and enjoy spending on social outings.

Libra and Capricorn

This is a *one-sided money relationship* where Capricorn has complete control over the finances. Libra recognizes Capricorn's need to be responsible for the financial plan. Libra can be disheartened by Capricorn's reluctance to spend money on social outings. Practical Capricorn is driven to be cautious with discretionary luxury purchases much to Libra's displeasure. Libra tends not to complain to keep the peace.

Libra and Aquarius

This can be a *harmonious money relationship.* Both parties are outgoing and like to spend money on social events. Neither are overly-concerned about financial security. Both value personal relationships more so than personal possessions; Libra is focused on a relationship with another individual and Sagittarius is focused on a relationship with groups of people.

Libra and Pisces

This is a *one-sided money relationship* with the responsibility of money issues falling by default to Libra to handle. Pisces has little desire to be involved with finances. Libra will take the time to weigh the pros and cons and sensibly carry out a financial plan that enables them to have a balanced lifestyle. Pisces is emotionally supportive of Libra's efforts.

♏

SCORPIO'S MONEY RELATIONSHIPS

Scorpio's Viewpoint: *"Money reveals the inner greed in people and their degree of caring for others."*

Scorpio and Aries

This could work as a *compensating money relationship.* See *'Aries and Scorpio'* described above.

Scorpio and Taurus

This can be a *harmonious money relationship.* See *'Taurus and Scorpio'* described above.

Scorpio and Gemini

This can be a *one-sided financial relationship.* See *'Gemini and Scorpio'* described above.

Scorpio and Cancer

This is a *harmonious money relationship.* See *'Cancer and Scorpio'* described above.

Scorpio and Leo

This is an *opposing money relationship.* See *'Leo and Scorpio'* described above.

Scorpio and Virgo

This is a *one-sided money relationship.* See *'Virgo and Scorpio'* described above.

Scorpio and Libra

This is a *one-sided money relationship.* See *'Libra and Scorpio'* described above.

Scorpio and Scorpio

This is a *harmonious money relationship.* This is a powerful meeting of intense minds that can undoubtedly overcome any financial obstacles and successfully reach their monetary goals. Both share similar desires and have a deep understanding of each others' needs and want to please each other.

Scorpio and Sagittarius

This is an *opposing money relationship.* Scorpio would like complete control of the finances but Sagittarius is not willing to relinquish the major money decisions to Scorpio. Sagittarius wants individual freedom to spend on personal wants. Scorpio admires Sagittarius' creativity yet is not fond of Sagittarius' adventuresome spending habits. Sagittarius is irritated by Scorpio's reluctance to be open with money maneuvers but trusts in Scorpio's good intentions.

Scorpio and Capricorn

This is a *harmonious money relationship* with both parties honoring each others monetary needs.   Both are determined and reliable individuals that value hard work to achieve their financial goals. They can formulate a financial plan together and firmly commit to carrying it out patiently over the course of time. They can easily overcome any obstacles to their financial success.

Scorpio and Aquarius

This is an *opposing money relationship* where Aquarius' need for financial autonomy goes against Scorpio's need for financial control. Aquarius can not bear Scorpio's tendency to bury personal money matters instead of being straight-forward and objectively discuss financial issues. Scorpio is suspicious of Aquarius' eccentric spending habits and is wary of inviting Aquarius' input into a financial plan.

Scorpio and Pisces

This is a *one-sided money relationship* with Scorpio in quiet control. Pisces feels secure with Scorpio at the helm and is confident that Scorpio will govern the financial plan with their best interests at heart. Pisces dutifully supports Scorpio's monetary goals. Scorpio appreciates Pisces' loyalty.

SAGITTARIUS' MONEY RELATIONSHIPS

Sagittarius' Viewpoint: *"Money is a positive force that lets me be free to explore my ultimate aspirations."*

Sagittarius and Aries

This can be a *harmonious money relationship.* See *'Aries and Sagittarius'* described above.

Sagittarius and Taurus

This can be a *compensating financial relationship.* See *'Taurus and Sagittarius'* described above.

Sagittarius and Gemini

This can be a *harmonious money relationship.* See *'Gemini and Sagittarius'* described above.

Sagittarius and Cancer

This is an *opposing money relationship.* See *'Cancer and Sagittarius'* described above.

Sagittarius and Leo

This is a *harmonious money relationship.* See *'Leo and Sagittarius'* described above.

Sagittarius and Virgo

This is an *opposing money relationship*. See *'Virgo and Sagittarius'* described above.

Sagittarius and Libra

This is a *harmonious money relationship.* See *'Libra and Sagittarius'* described above.

Sagittarius and Scorpio

This is an *opposing money relationship.* See *'Scorpio and Sagittarius'* described above.

Sagittarius and Sagittarius

This is a *harmonious money relationship* where both parties share similar ideals of freedom, optimism and generosity. It is difficult for these two to adhere to a rigid financial plan given their mutual love of spending on social activities, partaking in travel adventures and being generous to others. Both have great faith in positive life outcomes and invariably they end up wealthy. They are often in the right place at the right time for money opportunities and give validity to the expression, "Positive attracts positive".

Sagittarius and Capricorn

This is an *opposing money relationship*. When it comes to money matters, Capricorn wants the control and responsibility of financial decisions. Sagittarius recognizes Capricorn's practical sense of handling money issues and can yield to Capricorn on major financial decisions. Giving Capricorn complete control of their finances, though, would be too limiting on Sagittarius' spending desires. Capricorn is well aware of Sagittarius' appetite for spending on adventurous endeavors and finds it extravagant. There is less friction when both parties can tend to their own individual finances as long as Sagittarius doesn't jeopardize Capricorn's financial plan for the long run. In that case, Capricorn may no longer tolerate Sagittarius' freedom to spend and demand complete control.

Sagittarius and Aquarius

This is a *harmonious money relationship* where both parties respect individuality and freedom to spend as they please. Neither are petty and both have broad outlooks. Sagittarius' optimism and Aquarius' capacity to go beyond the ordinary can bode well for creative solutions to financial obstacles. Their social contacts will serve them well when seeking money-making opportunities. Neither want to attend to the mundane chore of adhering to a financial plan.

Sagittarius and Pisces

This is a *one-sided money relationship.* Sagittarius will be the one to initiate spending plans and Pisces will kindly adapt to be on-side with the plans. Pisces admires Sagittarius' high energy level and resilience when dealing with money matters. Pisces gently relinquishes the duty of financial management to Sagittarius and is sympathetic if things don't work out as well as the optimistic Sagittarius had planned.

CAPRICORN'S MONEY RELATIONSHIPS

Capricorn's Viewpoint: *"Money means power, the ability to get ahead in life and reach your goals."*

Capricorn and Aries

This can be a *compensating money relationship.* See *'Aries and Capricorn'* described above.

Capricorn and Taurus

This is a *harmonious money relationship.* See *'Taurus and Capricorn'* described above.

Capricorn and Gemini

This is a *one-sided money relationship.* See *'Gemini and Capricorn'* described above.

Capricorn and Cancer

This can be a *harmonious money relationship.* See *'Cancer and Capricorn'* described above.

Capricorn and Leo

This can be an *opposing money relationship.* See *'Leo and Capricorn'* described above.

Capricorn and Virgo

This is a *harmonious money relationship.* See *'Virgo and Capricorn'* described above.

Capricorn and Libra

This is a *one-sided money relationship.* See *'Libra and Capricorn'* described above.

Capricorn and Scorpio

This is a *harmonious money relationship.* See *'Scorpio and Capricorn'* described above.

Capricorn and Sagittarius

This is an *opposing money relationship.* See *'Sagittarius and Capricorn'* described above.

Capricorn and Capricorn

This is a *harmonious money relationship.* Both parties are deadly serious about money issues. It is highly likely that they will draw up a thorough financial plan that they will both commit to and work hard to achieve. Both are risk-adverse and are conservative spenders. They are also status-conscious and the possessions they acquire that are in the public's view reflect their high standards. They are both ambitious and will yield to each other in order to move the both of them further up the success ladder.

Capricorn and Aquarius

This is an *opposing money relationship.* Aquarius is far too independent for the likes of restricting Capricorn. Aquarius rebels against any limitations Capricorn places on their personal finances. As much as Capricorn would like to have Aquarius think 'inside the Capricorn box', it is improbable that Aquarius can willingly adapt to the money expectations of Capricorn. The only expectations that Aquarius can adapt to are those that are true to Aquarius' ideals.

Capricorn and Pisces

This is a *one-sided money relationship* with Capricorn in control of the personal finances and making the spending rules. Pisces follows along willingly, deeply aware of the strength of Capricorn's determination to arrive at their financial goals. Pisces will passionately support Capricorn's desire for success.

AQUARIUS' MONEY RELATIONSHIPS

Aquarius' Viewpoint: *"Money gives me the freedom to do what is right for the benefit of mankind."*

Aquarius and Aries

This can be an *opposing money relationship.* See *'Aries and Aquarius'* described above.

Aquarius and Taurus

This is a *one-sided money relationship.* See *'Taurus and Aquarius'* described above.

Aquarius and Gemini

This can be a *harmonious money relationship.* See *'Gemini and Aquarius'* described above.

Aquarius and Cancer

This is an *opposing money relationship.* See *'Cancer and Aquarius'* described above.

Aquarius and Leo

This is a *compensating money relationship.* See *'Leo and Aquarius'* described above.

Aquarius and Virgo

This can be an *opposing money relationship.* See *'Virgo and Aquarius'* described above.

Aquarius and Libra

This can be a *harmonious money relationship.* See *'Libra and Aquarius'* described above.

Aquarius and Scorpio

This is an *opposing money relationship.* See *'Scorpio and Aquarius'* described above.

Aquarius and Sagittarius

This is a *harmonious money relationship.* See *'Sagittarius and Aquarius'* described above.

Aquarius and Capricorn

This is an *opposing money relationship.* See *'Capricorn and Aquarius'* described above.

Aquarius and Aquarius

This is an *opposing money relationship* where both parties want to independently control their own finances. Both accept each others need to be free to do exactly what they want with their money. This acceptance is easier on them than having to make compromises. They are supportive of each others financial goals and are not possessive of their belongings. Neither party questions the rationale of eccentric purchases nor questions the amount of money spent on frequent social outings.

Aquarius and Pisces

This is a *one-sided money relationship* and by default, the onus of managing the finances falls on Aquarius. Aquarius has the logical and detached mind to make objective financial decisions and Pisces is happy to let Aquarius do so. Pisces finds the task of looking after money issues far too emotionally frustrating.

♓

PISCES' MONEY RELATIONSHIPS

Pisces' Viewpoint: *"Money can afford you the time to be able to dream and imagine the impossible."*

Pisces and Aries

This is a *one-sided money relationship.* See *'Aries and Pisces'* described above.

Pisces and Taurus

This is a *one-sided money relationship.* See *'Taurus and Pisces'* described above.

Pisces and Gemini

This is a *one-sided money relationship.* See *'Gemini and Pisces'* described above.

Pisces and Cancer

This is a *one-sided money relationship.* See *'Cancer and Pisces'* described above.

Pisces and Leo

This is a *one-sided money relationship.* See *'Leo and Pisces'* described above.

Pisces and Virgo

This can be an *opposing money relationship.* See *'Virgo and Pisces'* described above.

Pisces and Libra

This is a *one-sided money relationship.* See *'Libra and Pisces'* described above.

Pisces *and Scorpio*

This is a *one-sided money relationship.* See *'Scorpio and Pisces'* described above.

Pisces and Sagittarius

This is a *one-sided money relationship*. See *'Sagittarius and Pisces'* described above.

Pisces and Capricorn

This is a *one-sided money relationship*. See *'Capricorn and Pisces'* described above.

Pisces and Aquarius

This is a *one-sided money relationship*. See *'Aquarius and Pisces'* described above.

Pisces and Pisces

This is a *harmonious money relationship*. Both strive for serenity and are non-competitive. Money is rarely a point of contention between them. They both can imagine themselves in the others position and can easily comprehend the others point of view. They both will take the path of least resistance when it comes to money matters.

AN ENDING NOTE

The Dalai Lama, when asked what surprised him the most about humanity, answered, "Man. Because he sacrifices his health in order to make money. Then he sacrifices money to recuperate his health. And then he is so anxious about the future that he does not enjoy the present; the result being that he does not live in the present or the future; he lives as if he is never going to die, and then dies having never really lived."

Last words of advice: When you *know* you have arrived at a point in time where you have accumulated *enough* money such that you can live the rest of your potential life with the peace of mind that you are secure, then "make love, not work". Indulge in your passions and do what you love to do.